Who Is
Kamala Harris?

Who Is
Kamala Harris?

by Kirsten Anderson

illustrated by Manuel Gutierrez

Penguin Workshop

For Professor Garro—MG

PENGUIN WORKSHOP
An Imprint of Penguin Random House LLC, New York

Copyright © 2021 by Penguin Random House LLC. All rights reserved.
Published by Penguin Workshop, an imprint of Penguin Random House LLC, New York.
PENGUIN and PENGUIN WORKSHOP are trademarks of Penguin Books Ltd.
WHO HQ & Design is a registered trademark of Penguin Random House LLC.
Printed in the USA.

Visit us online at www.penguinrandomhouse.com.

Library of Congress Cataloging-in-Publication Data is available upon request.

ISBN 9780593384480 (paperback)   10 9 8 7 6 5 4 3 2 1
ISBN 9780593384497 (library binding)   10 9 8 7 6 5 4 3 2 1

Contents

Who Is Kamala Harris?

On August 11, 2020, a US senator from California named Kamala Harris tweeted: "Black women and women of color have long been underrepresented in elected office and in November we have an opportunity to change that. Let's get to work."

Three hours later, Democratic presidential candidate Joe Biden tweeted: "I have the great honor to announce that I've picked @KamalaHarris—a fearless fighter for the little guy, and one of the country's finest public servants—as my running mate."

Kamala Harris, the senator from California, had been selected to be the Democratic candidate for vice president. She was taking the opportunity to make the change she had just talked about.

The choice made sense in many ways. Kamala was an experienced politician. She had won several races for public office in her native California. She knew how to campaign. And she agreed with Joe Biden on many issues.

But even in 2020, his choice of Kamala was a bold move. There were still people who didn't believe a woman could hold a leadership position like vice president. Geraldine Ferraro and Sarah Palin had both run for vice president. Hillary Clinton had run for president. Kamala was only the fourth woman—and the first woman of color—to run at this level. Her father was Black and her mother was Indian. People weren't used to seeing someone that looked like her running for the second-highest office in the country.

Some people were thrilled by the news—including many women of color. If Kamala Harris could be nominated for vice president, then maybe things were changing for women, and especially for women of color.

Other voters had a more mixed reaction. They liked the fact that Kamala was a woman of color. They knew that it had taken far too long for a Black or Southeast Asian woman to get a chance to be in power. But they didn't think Kamala was willing to push hard enough for change on topics like health care or law enforcement.

Kamala knew there were doubters. But that was okay. She had been the first many times before. She had been the first Black woman district attorney in California. She had been the first Black woman to be elected attorney general of California. And she had been the first Black woman senator from California. She was used to fighting, so she was ready to fight doubt. And she was ready to fight for the American people.

CHAPTER 1
Shyamala and the Girls

Kamala Devi Harris was born in Oakland, California, on October 20, 1964. Her name means "lotus flower," an important symbol in Indian culture.

Kamala's father, Donald Harris, came from Jamaica to study economics at the University of California, Berkeley. Shyamala Gopalan, her mother, came to Berkeley from India. She studied nutrition and endocrinology. She later became a breast cancer researcher. Both of Kamala's parents were involved in the civil rights movement of the 1960s, and that's how they met. Kamala remembers riding along in her stroller at protests and marches. Friends from the civil rights movement became as close as family, and Kamala grew up listening to them discuss the fight for racial justice and how they could change the world.

Kamala's sister, Maya, was born in 1967. When Kamala was only seven years old, her parents decided to get divorced. Her father remained involved in her life. But it was her mother who raised Kamala and her sister. The three became very close.

Shyamala knew that most Americans would think of Kamala and Maya as Black women. She made sure that they were proud of their identity and that they were part of the Black community in Oakland. They spent a lot of time at Rainbow Sign, a cultural center that featured Black performers, speakers, and thinkers. They visited their father's family in Jamaica as well.

But Shyamala also kept Kamala and Maya in touch with their Indian roots. Family members from India came to visit them in California, and the girls also traveled to India a few times. Kamala's grandfather had been part of the fight for India's independence from Britain and had held high-level government posts. When she visited him in India, she would listen as he and his friends talked about politics. Her Indian grandmother worked to improve the lives of women in rural villages.

Shyamala and the girls settled into an apartment in Berkeley, a city on the border of Oakland. Their neighborhood was mostly made up of working-class Black families. Kamala rode a bus to Thousand Oaks Elementary School, which was located in a wealthier part of Berkeley. She didn't know it at the time, but the bus ride was part of a national effort to integrate local schools. *Integrate* means to blend together. The idea was to bring kids from different races and classes together in schools. Because of the busing plan, Kamala went to a school with students from many types of backgrounds. She got to know people she might not have met without this plan.

After school, Kamala and Maya often went to a neighbor's house until their mother came home from work at her research lab. Kamala took piano lessons and went to dance classes as well.

At night, her mother loved to cook. She experimented with different recipes and found ways to make food fun. Kamala learned from her and became an excellent cook herself.

When Kamala was twelve, Shyamala was offered an important job in Montreal, Canada. Kamala didn't want to leave her friends and neighborhood in Berkeley. But it was an exciting opportunity for her mother. They all bought winter coats, boots, and gloves and set off for Canada.

In Montreal, many people speak French. Shyamala sent Kamala and Maya to a French-speaking school, but Kamala found it difficult. It was hard enough moving to a different country. Trying to settle in while learning a new language made it harder.

Another problem was their new apartment building. Kamala and Maya discovered that kids weren't allowed to play soccer on the building's lawn. They thought this was unfair! The sisters protested in front of the building. Soon enough, the building changed its rules. The power of protest had worked.

Kamala switched to a fine arts school and was much happier there. She learned to play the violin, French horn, and kettle drum. By the time she got to high school, she had settled into life in Montreal and even joined an all-girl dance troupe known as Super Six. But when it was time for college, she was ready to return to the United States.

CHAPTER 2
For the People

After graduating from high school in 1981, Kamala entered Howard University in Washington, DC. Howard is an HBCU (Historically Black College and University). Kamala loved Howard immediately. She found it exciting to be surrounded by so many brilliant and creative young people of color. She was on the debate team and became a member of a sorority, Alpha Kappa Alpha.

In 1986, Kamala graduated from Howard with a degree in political science and economics. She decided to become a lawyer and returned to California to attend the University of California, Hastings College of the Law in San Francisco, near where she had grown up in Berkeley.

HBCUs
(Historically Black Colleges and Universities)

In the early 1800s, there weren't many colleges in the United States that would accept Black students. In response, colleges built specifically for Black students began to appear. The first was the African Institute (now Cheyney University), which was established in 1837 in Pennsylvania. Others followed, with many founded in the years following the Civil War, including Howard University, Morehouse College, Hampton University, and Tuskegee University. Today there are over a hundred HBCUs.

Among other qualifications, the Higher Education Act of 1965 defined an HBCU as "any historically black college or university that was established prior to 1964, whose principal mission

Howard University

was, and is, the education of black Americans."
Although HBCUs are mainly focused on providing
opportunities to Black students, they are open to
students of any race and ethnicity.

At Hastings, she realized that she wanted to become a prosecutor and work in a district attorney's office.

A prosecutor usually works for a city or state government. Prosecutors decide whether someone should be charged with a crime. They try to convince a jury that the person charged with the crime is guilty. The district attorney (DA) is the chief prosecutor for a specific area. District attorneys are usually elected by local voters.

Many family members and friends weren't happy about Kamala's decision. They believed that prosecutors often were harder on people of color. Innocent people of color had been put in jail by prosecutors who were more interested in closing a case than finding justice.

Kamala saw it differently. As a Black woman, she understood that there were problems with the judicial, or court, system. But that's why she felt she had to get involved. She wanted to try to change the system. And by doing so, she could change the lives of people in her community.

After graduating from law school in 1989, Kamala was offered a job as a deputy district attorney in the Alameda County District Attorney's Office in Oakland. First, however, she had to take a test called the bar exam. Anyone who wants to be a lawyer has to pass this very difficult test. Test results usually aren't known for months.

Kamala started her new job, but then she got some unexpected news. She had failed the bar exam.

She was horribly embarrassed. She kept her job but couldn't take on her own cases in a courtroom. Kamala was miserable.

In February 1990, she took the exam again. This time she passed. Kamala was relieved and thrilled to finally start her career.

Kamala now could walk into a courtroom and argue a case. As a prosecutor, she introduced herself as "Kamala Harris, for the people." That always reminded Kamala that she was there to represent the people in her area.

In 1998, Kamala took a job with the San Francisco District Attorney's Office. It was an important job in one of America's biggest cities, but she found the office was very disorganized. There weren't enough computers. Files weren't taken care of. More than a dozen lawyers were fired suddenly. Some cases weren't even being brought to trial.

Kamala left the San Francisco DA's office after eighteen months. Then she went to work in the San Francisco City Attorney's Office, working on programs that would help young people who had been abused.

In 2003, the current San Francisco district attorney was up for reelection. Kamala decided to run against him. They were both Democrats. He was very well known. She was not. But Kamala felt the office should be better run. It was time for her to step in and take charge.

CHAPTER 3
DA

Kamala set up her campaign headquarters in the Bayview, a struggling San Francisco neighborhood. There weren't many jobs, and the buildings were in bad condition. Campaign experts had told Kamala that she would never be able to get volunteers to come to a "dangerous neighborhood" to help her. But Kamala insisted on it. She wanted to make a point. If she was elected district attorney, she would be there for everyone. That included the poorer people in communities like the Bayview who were often ignored.

The campaign experts turned out to be wrong. Volunteers from all over the city, even from the wealthiest areas, came to the Bayview to help Kamala.

Meanwhile, Kamala wanted to meet as many people as possible. She could often be found outside busy locations like grocery stores, talking to shoppers and giving out material that explained her campaign positions. Instead of a table, she would spread out her campaign literature on an ironing board. She thought the ironing board made a great standing desk. And it certainly caught people's eyes.

Kamala won the race. On January 8, 2004, she became the first woman and first person of color elected as San Francisco's district attorney. After she won, Kamala went to her new office and made a list of things she wanted to do.

Some of them were simple things, like painting the office and getting new computers. Others were harder. She pushed the prosecutors in the office to try to close murder cases. Kamala wanted families of murder victims to get justice.

But Kamala also wanted to make sure that the court system wasn't too hard on people who committed minor crimes. During her years as a prosecutor, she had seen how being

arrested for a low-level crime could turn the rest of someone's life in the wrong direction.

In 2005, Kamala created a program called Back on Track. People who were charged with

low-level, nonviolent crimes could enter the program. They had to meet certain goals. They attended school full-time, did community service, and went to counseling. If they made it through the program, the charges for their crime would be dropped and they would have a clean record.

Back on Track was very successful. Few of the people who graduated from the program committed crimes again. Other states and cities adopted similar programs.

People didn't always agree with Kamala's other choices, though. When a police officer was shot and killed in the Bayview, Kamala decided not to pursue the death penalty for the officer's murderer. That turned many people against her.

Her anti-truancy program also upset people. A high number of students in San Francisco weren't going to school. (That's called truancy.)

As a prosecutor, Kamala had noticed that many people who became involved in crime hadn't finished school. She thought that it might be possible to cut down on crime by keeping kids in school. Kamala's program involved steps where support services tried to help families where a student was missing a lot of school days. If that didn't work, the case could be sent to the DA's office. Then the parents could be fined or possibly even serve time in jail.

Some people were not comfortable with this program. They thought the legal system shouldn't get involved in a family and school issue. Other people felt that it unfairly targeted families who were already struggling. The program didn't take their problems into account.

But Kamala thought it was important. She described her programs as being "smart on crime." And enough voters agreed. She was elected to a second term as San Francisco district attorney.

CHAPTER 4
First and First

In 2008, Kamala received terrible news. Her mother, Shyamala, had been diagnosed with cancer. She died in 2009.

The loss was extremely difficult for Kamala. She had been very close to her mother. Kamala had been inspired by her mother's strength and felt that much of her success had come from the way her mother had raised her. She knew she would never stop missing her.

In 2010, Kamala ran for attorney general of California. A state attorney general advises the state government on all legal matters. The attorney general also represents the legal interests of the people of the state in a wide variety of cases on topics like internet crimes, election fraud, environmental laws, violent crimes, and even child support.

Many people didn't think Kamala had a chance. Not many women had served as a state's attorney general. And there had been even fewer Black attorneys general. Kamala was running against a well-known Republican who had been the Los Angeles district attorney.

The election took place on November 2, 2010. But the voting was too close to call. They would have to wait until all the ballots were counted.

The counting dragged on for weeks. People constantly asked Kamala when it would be over. But she didn't know.

It was almost Thanksgiving. As Kamala was boarding a flight to New York to spend the holiday with her sister and her family, she got a phone call. All the votes had been counted.

And she had won. Kamala became the first woman and first person of color to be elected attorney general of California.

Kamala took office on January 3, 2011. And she had one very big issue to deal with right away. The United States had been suffering from a financial crisis since 2008. Many people had lost their jobs. And now they were losing their houses.

An investigation found that large numbers of homeowners had bought houses they couldn't really afford. Banks and housing lenders created mortgages (home loans) that were to their advantage. They then found ways to force people out of their own homes.

The banks wanted to settle the case quickly. They offered each state money to share with the people who had lost their homes. Kamala knew people's lives had been ruined by the housing crisis. She thought they deserved more money than what the banks had offered. Other state attorneys general joined her fight. Finally, the banks gave in. Kamala won $25 billion for

Californians who had been affected by the crisis.

Kamala had many accomplishments as attorney general. She took her Back on Track program statewide. And she led the creation of OpenJustice, a database that made information about crime and police activity open to the public.

But not everyone was happy with Kamala. When she expanded her San Francisco anti-truancy program to the entire state, some parents ended up serving time in jail. People felt that she had turned a family problem into a crime. Others felt that she didn't do enough to fight police brutality or reform California's overcrowded prisons.

But Kamala was elected to a second term as attorney general of California in 2014. And she celebrated another big event that same year: her marriage to Doug Emhoff.

A friend had introduced Kamala to Doug, a Los Angeles lawyer, in 2013. They knew quickly that they wanted to be together, and they were married on August 22, 2014. Doug had two children from a previous marriage, Cole and Ella. Kamala was overjoyed by her new family and settled into life with them. She loved to cook and created a new tradition where the family had a big dinner together every Sunday.

In 2016, Kamala took another major step forward when she ran as a Democrat for the US Senate. She won the election and became the first woman of color to serve as senator from California. She was the second Black woman elected to the US Senate and the first South Asian woman to hold a senate seat.

As senator, Kamala worked to protect immigrants and supported plans to address climate change in the United States.

But Kamala would become best known for her smart questioning of people brought before senate committees. Her experience as a prosecutor showed during these sessions. People took notice of Kamala. They saw her as someone who was tough and clear thinking.

Kamala would need those qualities for her next step: a run for the US presidency.

CHAPTER 5
Veep

On January 27, 2019, Kamala launched her presidential campaign from her hometown of Oakland, California. Around twenty thousand people listened as she spoke about the problems faced by Americans at that time and how she planned to help solve them.

It was a great start to Kamala's campaign. Election watchers called her one of the favorites to win the Democratic nomination.

But more and more Democrats announced that they were also running for the chance to be the Democratic nominee for president. Soon, there were over twenty candidates!

The first debate took place in June 2019.

Kamala spoke up about an issue that was

important to her personally. She noted that another candidate, former vice president Joe Biden, had argued against laws that would allow students from poor neighborhoods to be bused to schools in wealthier neighborhoods.

Kamala said: "There was a little girl in California who was part of the second class to integrate her public schools. She was bused to school every day. That little girl was me."

Kamala spoke with a passion that electrified

the crowd. It showed voters how she had been personally affected by lawmakers' decisions and that she knew how their lives could be changed by laws, too.

The clip of that moment at the debate went viral. Kamala's campaign raised millions of dollars in the days after the debate. Polls showed her gaining ground on the leaders in the race.

But it was hard for anyone to stand out from the large crowd. Candidates like Joe Biden and Senator Bernie Sanders from Vermont were well known. They easily got attention. Some were very progressive candidates. They promised big changes, like health care for all and free college. Others were more moderate. They also promised changes, but more slowly and through smaller steps.

Kamala found herself somewhere in between those groups. She was progressive in some areas and moderate in others. People couldn't sum her up easily.

Kamala continued to do well in the debates. She worked hard at getting out and meeting voters. But it became difficult to raise money for her campaign.

On December 3, 2019, Kamala announced that she was ending her campaign. In March 2020, she announced that she would vote for Joe Biden. He went on to become the Democratic presidential nominee.

After Joe Biden pledged to select a female vice president, his campaign team spent months interviewing respected women politicians for the position. They knew that he was looking for someone with experience who could handle the job.

Kamala was one of the women they interviewed. Although they had clashed during the debates, Kamala knew Joe personally. She had always gotten along with him.

On August 11, Joe Biden called Kamala to

offer her the opportunity to join his presidential campaign as the candidate for vice president. She accepted, and the announcement was made

a few hours later. That day, Kamala became another "first" for the history books: the first woman of color to run for vice president for a major political party.

Kamala's mother had always told her, "You may be the first, but don't be the last." She meant that Kamala should try to help other women who followed in her path so that soon there would be more of them in important positions, and people would no longer need to be counting firsts.

As Kamala set out on the campaign trail in her Converse sneakers, she knew there was a lot more work to do. There were plenty of people whose voices needed to be heard. And she could change that. It started with just being out there on the campaign trail. It started with showing that she could take on a role that once had been closed to women and people of color. It started with showing other women and people of color that they, too, had a powerful voice and were seen.

On November 7, 2020, it was announced that Joe Biden and Kamala Harris had won the election. Kamala would be the first woman of color to serve in one of the most powerful positions in the government. In a speech after the election announcement, Kamala had a message to the young people of the world. She said that they should dream about what they knew they could do, not what others said they could do. Kamala told them to "see yourself in a way that others might not see you, simply because they've never seen it before. And we will applaud you every step of the way."

Once again, Kamala was the first. But she was ready to make sure she wasn't the last.

Timeline of Kamala Harris's Life

1964 — Kamala Harris is born October 20 in Oakland, California

1971 — Parents decide to divorce

1976 — Moves to Montreal

1986 — Graduates from Howard University

1989 — Earns law degree from Hastings College

1990 — Becomes a deputy district attorney in Oakland

1998 — Joins San Francisco District Attorney's Office

2003 — Elected San Francisco district attorney

2005 — Creates Back on Track program for San Francisco

2009 — Mother dies from colon cancer

2010 — Elected California attorney general

2014 — Marries Douglas Emhoff

2016 — Elected US senator from California

2019 — Declares candidacy for president in January; exits race in December

2020 — Selected as candidate for vice president by Joe Biden in August; elected vice president of the United States in November

Timeline of the World

1964 — The Civil Rights Act is passed in the United States

1968 — Martin Luther King Jr. is assassinated

1969 — Neil Armstrong becomes the first human to walk on the moon

1973 — The Sydney Opera House opens in Australia

1979 — The Susan B. Anthony dollar coin is introduced

1980 — The Rubik's Cube puzzle is released worldwide

1986 — Halley's Comet appears for the first time in seventy-six years

1992 — The Mall of America opens in Bloomington, Minnesota

1996 — IBM's Deep Blue computer defeats chess champion Garry Kasparov

2000 — The London Eye, the world's tallest Ferris wheel at the time, opens

2004 — A social networking site for Harvard students, later known as Facebook, is launched

2008 — Swimmer Michael Phelps wins eight gold medals at the Summer Olympics, the most gold medals won by one athlete at a single Olympics

2011 — The Occupy Wall Street protests against income inequality begin in New York

2016 — The game *Pokémon GO* is released

2020 — Basketball legend Kobe Bryant and his daughter Gianna die in a helicopter accident in California

Bibliography

Bruinius, Harry. "In Kamala Harris's richly textured background, a portrait of America today." *Christian Science Monitor*, August 19, 2020. https://www.csmonitor.com/USA/Politics/2020/0819/In-Kamala-Harris-richly-textured-background-a-portrait-of-America-today.

Burns, Alexander, Astead W. Herndon, and Jonathan Martin. "How Kamala Harris's Campaign Unraveled." *New York Times*, November 29, 2019. https://www.nytimes.com/2019/11/29/us/politics/kamala-harris-2020.html.

Egelko, Bob. "Harris' record as California attorney general could become issue in presidential race." *San Francisco Chronicle*, August 24, 2020. https://www.sfchronicle.com/politics/article/Harris-record-as-California-attorney-general-15508824.php.

Goodyear, Dana. "Kamala Harris Makes Her Case." *New Yorker*, July 15, 2019. https://www.newyorker.com/magazine/2019/07/22/kamala-harris-makes-her-case.

Harris, Kamala. *The Truths We Hold: An American Journey*. New York: Penguin Books, 2019.

Harris, Rachel L. "Kamala Harris's Nomination Is Everything to Me." *New York Times*, August 15, 2020. https://www.nytimes.com/2020/08/15/opinion/kamala-harris-vice-president-biden.html.

Kim, Catherine, and Zack Stanton. "55 Things You Need to Know About Kamala Harris." *Politico*, August 11, 2020. https://www.politico.com/news/magazine/2020/08/11/kamala-harris-vp-background-bio-biden-running-mate-2020-393885.

Lightman, David. "Kamala Harris in California: Big winner but a polarizing figure." *Sacramento Bee*, August 11, 2020. https://www.sacbee.com/news/politics-government/election/presidential-election/article244639912.html.

Lopez, German. "Kamala Harris's controversial record on criminal justice, explained." *Vox*, August 12, 2020. https://www.vox.com/future-perfect/2019/1/23/18184192/kamala-harris-president-campaign-criminal-justice-record.

Sitrin, Carly. "5 things Sen. Kamala Harris has done besides be interrupted." *Vox*, June 16, 2017. https://www.vox.com/policy-and-politics/2017/6/16/15808396/kamala-harris-democrat-rising-star-interrupted.

Summers, Juana. "Howard University Shaped Kamala Harris' Path to Political Heights." *Morning Edition*. NPR, August 19, 2020. https://www.npr.org/2020/08/19/903716274/howard-university-shaped-kamala-harris-path-to-political-heights.